# That You May Be Rich: Biblical teachings on Business, Finances and Wealth.

# Author: Tapiwa Chidakwa

## Contents

Background ........................................................................................................... 2

Bible characters who were rich .............................................................................. 3

Money is NOT evil, but greed is ............................................................................. 8

Debt is a form of slavery ........................................................................................ 9

Leaving an Inheritance for your children ............................................................. 11

God gives the power to make wealth .................................................................. 12

Whose does it all belong to? ............................................................................... 13

We all belong to him ........................................................................................... 14

He that observes the wind shall not reap ............................................................ 15

There is equal opportunity for all ........................................................................ 17

Heavens will open ............................................................................................... 18

The first command given to Adam ...................................................................... 19

Without vision people perish .............................................................................. 21

Heaven is rich ...................................................................................................... 22

God shall supply your every need ....................................................................... 23

**Parable of the Talents** (Matthew 25 Vs 14 – 30) ............................................. 24

Conclusion ........................................................................................................... 25

# Background

Looking at my background, I can almost confirm with absolute certainty that Christians view rich people as sinners who are not worth of heaven. I can testify that in most of the church services that I have attended there is hardly a time when I heard the preacher stand up and talk about whether God wants his children to enjoy the riches of the earth. It almost sounds like a taboo to speak good about money when you are in church. In comparing that with other Pentecostal churches that I have watched on TV, some of them seem to go strong on the gospel of prosperity and nothing much about the gospel and the word of God. These two scenarios are truly confusing to Christians who is still growing in faith. The big question that arises is 'Does God want you to get rich?"

I have spent the most part of my life in a Christian set up, my family is a Christian family and I was sent to a Christian boarding school. The values that were instilled in me during this entire period made resent and despise the rich and made me want to question a lot on what God had to say about this subject. It's as if church was making it hard for Christians, much like it wants Christians to choose between being rich or going to heaven. Do I really have to choose between being rich or going to heaven? Can't I be rich on earth and still go to heaven? Does wealth actually come from God? So I began a search of the scriptures on these particular issues and found quit a number of scriptures and verses that were so significant that I had to write this book and share with you what I found out.

My findings indicated that the bible does not only talk about the kingdom of heaven only, neither is it a source of comfort, inspiration only nor is it a simple guide on how to conduct ourselves. The bible also has a whole lot of wisdom to guide Christians on issues to do with money and wealth creation. Believe you me, I found out that it is not a gloomy picture at all. The fact that you are reading this book indicates that you are keen to know God's position regarding wealth and Christianity as well and I will share with you what I have found out. After my extensive study of the bible I began to view the bible in a totally different light. I couldn't believe that a book that was written so many years ago could be very useful in addressing today's problems about money and wealth. Thus right, the bible had brilliant and timeless answers to these issues. God does care about us and he wants us to understand these concepts. It even altered the way I viewed life and challenged me to do even more with my life. I had to make a decision to break from the exhausting cycle of living from pay check to pay check, trying so hard to make ends meet and constantly coming up shot.

Let's face it, money is important to everyone Christians and non-Christians alike. We both need it and use it on a daily basis to transact and to solve some issues we meet that require money.

God is more committed to our success than we are. Our success is important to God. Very manufacturer who makes a product makes sure that everything that is necessary for its successful functioning is in place. On top of that a product manual is written and enclosed in the shipping package together with the product. The product manual is for the user to read in order to acquaint himself on how to successfully use it. The bible is the product manual that should help us to succeed. The bible is written with a whole lot of instructions that we will need to read in order to succeed. Just like the manufacturer, God is very concerned with the success of the product, since the first thing he put on us is his image. All that we are going to all at is derived from the manual which was given for us to use.

When it comes to possessions, there are three groups of people that exist in life, the poor, the rich and the wealth. Poverty is lack of access to the resources you need in life, rich people are those that have accumulate excess resources on the other hand the wealth produce whatever they need when they need it. Wealthy people don't care what the economic environment looks like. Good or bad they can still create the environment they want and find the means to produce what they want. For purposes of this book we are going to use wealth and riches interchangeably.

## Bible characters who were rich

In my research I came across several people who were rich and still found favour with God and served him. Some of these people are common to most Christians but not much emphasis is projected on their earthly possessions. Of course back then riches and wealth were measure in a few different ways which might or might not be familiar in the present day practice. Back then people could possess actual gold and silver (a true storage of wealth), vast of land cattle, sheep goats and other domestic animals. I will share with you what I found about these people, their riches and relationship with God.

### Abraham (Genesis 13)

*Genesis 13 vs. 2 "And Abram was very rich in Cattle, in silver and in Gold"*

Abraham who was blessed by God to become the father of many nations had in his possession lots cattle, gold and silver as we can depict from the above verse. At one point he had to share his possessions with his nephew Lot as a result of disputes that arose.

*Vs.15 "for the land which thou seest, to thee will I give it, and to thy seed forever"*

*Vs16 "and I will make thy seed as the dust of the earth....."*

The verses above are showing the promises of blessing that God made to Abram. In verse 15 the Lord was promising to bless him with more wealth and in verse 16 he was promising to bless him with abundance of decadence.

## Isaac (Genesis 26)

*Genesis 26 vs.3 "....... And I will be with thee & I will bless thee, for unto thee, and unto thy seed, I will give all these countries....."*

*Vs.12 "then Isaac sowed in that land and received in the same year an hundred fold: and the Lord blessed him."*

*Vs.14 "for he had possession of flock, and possession of herds and great store of servants: and the Philistines envied him."*

In verse 3 of chapter 26 Isaac got a blessing from the Lord, much like the one his father Abraham got. He went and dwelt in a foreign land as per the Lord's instruction. In that foreign land the Lord was with him, he continued to bless the works of his hands; to a point where he became so powerful and wealthy such that even the Philistines envied him.

## Job (Job 1)

*Job 1 vs. 3 "His substance also was seven thousand sheep, and three thousand camels, and five hundred yoke of oxen and five hundred she asses, and a very great household: so that this man was the greatest of all the men of the east."*

Job became so wealth to the point where he held a record of being the richest man in the east.

*Vs. 8 "And the Lord said unto Satan, Hast thou considered my servant job, that there is none like him in the earth, a perfect and an upright man, one that feareth God and escheweth evil?"*

Verse 8 is shows how proud God was with his servant Job. He was wealthy and he feared the evil. The Lord however allowed the devil to test Job. In the process he lost everything and became a miserable person, but later on the Lord restored his wealth and even doubled the wealth that he had lost prior

*Vs. 12 "So the Lord blessed the latter end of Job more than his beginning: for he had fourteen thousand sheep, and six thousand camels, and a thousand yoke of oxen, and a thousand she asses."*

Notice how at the end of his life Job was given twice the possession he had in the beginning. Imagine how he held the record for being the wealthiest man in the east; he now broke it as he became twice what he was in the beginning.

### Solomon (1 Kings) (2 Chronicles)

*1 Kings 1 vs. 13 "And I have also given thee that which thou hast not asked, both riches and honour; so that there shall not be any among the kings like unto thee all thy days."*

*2 Chronicles 9 vs. 13 " Now the weight of gold that came to Solomon in one year was six hundred and threescore and six talents of gold."*

*Vs.14 "...... and all the kings of Arabia and governors of the country brought gold and silver to Solomon."*

*Vs.22 "and King Solomon passed the kings of the earth in riches and wisdom."*

*V. 27 "And the king made silver in Jerusalem as stones..."*

Solomon made a wise decision and asked for wisdom but he did not only have wisdom as we know him by, he had it all. On top of the wisdom and the numerous women in his life, he had gold and silver coming to him in unimaginable quantities. He was so rich to the extent that rumours of him triggered curiosity in queen of Sheba who had to come and see for herself.

The riches and wisdom were so much that he surpassed all other kings on earth. The bible itself says silver literally lost value to Solomon as he made it look like stones. It is this same Solomon who was tasked by God to build a temple for the Lord. He probably tasked him to build this temple because he was able to. He had the resources sufficient to construct a temple of the Lord.

Solomon became rich through four primary ways that are stated in 2 Chronicles chapter 9. He was involved in commerce and trade and ships of Tarshish would constantly bring gold, silver, ivory, apes and peacocks (vs. 21). He also got gift (vs. 9). Other kings would also pay tribute (vs. 24). Finally he also taxed his subordinates which he reigned over. While it might be a bit difficult for us to estimate how rich

Solomon was exactly, a rough calculation done by other researchers and bible students indicate that an estimate of 1.1 billion dollars' worth of gold was received by Solomon every year. This exclude the wealth he inherited from his father David and tributes and taxes. The argument to this day motions that Solomon was and still is the wealthiest human to ever walk the surface of the earth.

The bible is full of example of such characters. While we might not be able to exhaust the list and adequately examine each and every one of them, I will simply provide a list for you to further research on at your own convenience. Both the old and new testaments are full of rich followers of the Lord.

Joseph (Genesis) – the rags to riches story. He was good with money and he became second fiddle in Egypt responsible for the economy and finance. Joseph also called Barnabas (Acts 4:36-37); Dorcas (Acts 9:36); Cornelius (Acts 10:1); Sergius Paulus (Acts 13:6-12); Lydia (Acts 16:14-15); Jason (Acts 17:5-9); Aquila and Priscilla (Acts 18:2-3); Mnason of Cyprus (Acts 21:16) and finally Philemon (Philemon 1).

Having looked at these bible characters and the wealth they amassed it is safe for us to give an answer to the question "Can we live as straight forward and upright Christians and still be wealthy? The answer is a big YES WE CAN! All these people we handpicked from the bible lived faithful and upright lives and still managed to acquire and enjoy wealth. Most of these characters, if not all also gave generously. This is a responsibility placed upon Christians given that they are blessed by the Lord and serve as a conduit through which the Lord passes his blessing for the service of mankind. God expects us to work in his vineyard and serve others; it becomes more bearable if we have the wealth resources to expend in his work. But yet again the concept of philanthropy and generous giving is a topic on its own which is out of the context of this book.

That being said, it is important to note that inasmuch as Jesus talks harshly about the rich, saying it is harder for them to enter the kingdom of heaven than for a camel to go through the eye of a needle, it doesn't mean that it's impossible. Many wealthy people will make it to heaven if they follow what is required of them by God. Not all rich people are evil in the same way as not all poor people are righteous. Poverty is not a guarantee of virtue, and in the same manner wealth is not a guarantee of vice or moral weakness.

## Money is NOT evil, but greed is

When asked to define what money is, a simple definition would be "money is a medium of exchange'. It is used as legal tender that facilitates trade. People tend to misquote the bible and say "money is the root of all evil' this is not what the bible says. So what does the bible say about money. If it was so evil, then Christians should not even touch it or even get close to it if they intend to make it to heaven. So in of itself, money is not evil.

***1 Timothy 6 vs. 10 "For the love of money is the root of all evil. And some people: Which while some coveted after, they have erred from the faith, and pierced themselves through with many sorrows.***

In other words money is simply a tool for us to use to enable use to transact in the earthly kingdom. The only bad aspect is when you make it the master in your life and you crave for it and worship it. The bible state that when you start craving for money that is an indication of the root of evil. This craving can lead a person to do really bad thing for money. In this day and age we live in period where people kill for money; they commit adultery and fornicate for money. They lie, steal or cheat for the sake of money. These are just but a few of the evil deeds people commit all for the love of money.

Money will not make you a good or bad person; rather it magnifies more of what you already are. Individuals are encouraged to guard their thoughts and morality jealously. Money simply follows the character of the person whose hands it is in. when in the hands of a person who has good bible financial fundamentals, good things can only come out of it. On the other hand when an unhealthy craving for money becomes the core desire, then money becomes an idol or a mini god whom all attention and 'worship' is given. Unhealthy craving for money will result in an unquenchable desire for more and engaging in barbaric acts just to get it by any means necessary. Hence it can be concluded that money is an obedient servant and a bad master.

## Debt is a form of slavery

*Proverbs 22 vs.7 "The rich ruleth over the poor and the borrower is servant to the lender."*

The book of Proverbs is a collection of proverbs from the lips of King Solomon himself. We can recall that he asked for wisdom from the Lord and he was favoured not only with wisdom but with riches and honour, he was favoured by God. God does not what his children to be enslaved and be kept under bondage to anything. His inspiration to King Solomon gives us an insight of how debt enslaves the borrower. When one shackles himself in the golden "handcuffs of debt", he gives away part of his freedom to the lender. God wants his children to live in freedom.

God wants his children to live a life of abundance. It was never his intention for his children to suffer, but rather as a result of sin, the devil took advantage and used lack, scarcity and poverty to divert and capture souls for his own kingdom. When God created the earth in *Genesis 1 vs.28* he gave a mandate to man and said *"...be fruitful and multiply, and replenish the earth and subdue it"*

Debt in the form of home equity loans, credit cards, car loans, student loans and any other borrowing for extravagant lifestyles are among the most unbearable debts that are enslaving people in the modern day society. According to a study done by Bloomberg, student loan surpassed other forms of debts such as credit card, car loans and even home loans in some cases. The assumptions about future earnings have caused people to borrow recklessly and become slaves in the process as they work themselves to death trying to pay off their dues. After taking into consideration the principle amount plus the interest component, the settlement is close to two even three times of what was initially borrowed.

It is import to note however that debt is not a sin. Nowhere in the bible is it ever written that debt is a sin. The bible just gives words of advice for uptake by those who wish to take heed. Hence it further goes on to say "let he who has ears listen". There is no chapter in the book of Proverbs which goes without making use of phrases such as take heed, let him who has ears hear, hear these words, attend unto my wisdom, keep my words or a wise man will hear and increase knowledge and understanding. In this context King Solomon is advocating that getting into debt is simply biblically unwise.

There are other people who seem to manage debt very well and are capable of using it to leverage the grown and expansion of their business. Please note that I do not advocate that what they are doing is bad. One of my favourite authors of all time Robert and Kim Kiyosaki popularly known for the Rich Dad Poor Dad series of books are immensely wealthy. Donald Trump, the current president of the United State of America and a real estate mogul in his own right is also immensely wealth. All these great people have managed to build great empires using debt. To avoid confusion and improve our financial IQ, Robert Kiyosaki makes a clear distinction between good debt and bad debt. The good kind of debt of-course is the one that is productive and yield positive cash flow whilst the bad kind of debt being the one that is unproductive and doesn't yield any positive cash flow but simply accumulate interest.

Having established that there are two kinds of debt, good debt and bad debt and that it is not a sin but rather biblically unwise to be in debt, it is prudent for you to do everything you can to get yourself out of bad debt and accumulate good debt only where and when it is necessary to do so. There are several programs available out there to help you get out of debt.

# Leaving an Inheritance for your children

***Proverbs 13: 22 "A good man leaves an inheritance to his children's children."***

A wise man will hear these words from King Solomon. Parents are always trying to improve the lives of their children. They do not want them to go through the same hardships that they grew up under. It is only honourable for good parents to want to leave something behind for their children to inherit should they pass on. It is only possible to leave an inheritance for someone if you have made surpluses during your lifetime.

Inheritances are in many forms. Materially we are considering land, houses, antiques, family businesses, collectibles and even book. Financially we are considering quantities of money which will vary depending on how well one managed to work and generate money. There are other inheritances too that could be left behind for future generations. Reputation, character, legacy, genetics are other things that that could be passed on to other generations. The scope of this book will focus on material and financial inheritances.

Only the rich and wealthy write a will to distribute their possessions after death, poor people leave behind debts that will haunt their offspring for a long time after they are gone. Ask yourself a question, 'would you want your children to suffer after are gone, trying to pay off the debts that you incurred whilst you walked the surface of the earth?' If you are a good parent then the answer is NO! No one would want that for their children. What kind of a parent would that make you? Amass riches for your family whilst you are still alive so that when you depart they have something to hold on to.

The President of Kenya, Uhuru Kenyatta gave a bitter truth statement and said "if you really love your children, get a business, not a job, because when you die your children cannot inherit your job but they can definitely inherit your business. In fact, if you die on the job, your boss will replace you before your burial. If your family live in a company house, they will they will be kicked out before they ca say anything. So when you close from work, don't go and watch television. Go home and think of a business idea." These are bitter words to hear but they are the truth. No one is indispensable from their job. Companies can easily replace you and move forward without you.

There are several ways one can leave an inheritance for their children or children's children, depending on success. Some of the commonly used was include will writing, making use of trusts, making annual gifting to the intended beneficiaries or making use of estate.

## God gives the power to make wealth

***Deuteronomy 8 vs. 18 "But thou should remember the Lord your God; for it is he that gives the power to make wealth."***

Have you ever stopped for a moment and asked yourself where the power to amass wealth comes from? Well wonder no more. The bible makes it clear that the Lord God himself is the one that gives the power to make wealth. It is your obligation to always remind yourself that you on your own do not have the capability to get wealth. Vs. 17 of the same chapter is cautioning against bragging and being boastful that you have gotten wealthy by your own strength.

All we knew about growing up was to pray for every problem that came our way. If it was illness, the solution was to prayer for the illness to go away, if it was lack of money in the house, the solution was to pray for the money from God. More often than not the problems never really seem to disappear. The verse clearly indicates that God does not give you the wealth but rather he gives you the ability to make wealth. It is you now, with the ability given to you by God to create the wealth that you require. And hence the limit is your imagination as to how much wealth you make for your family.

Looking at the dictionary for the meaning of ability, I came up with several definitions of what it meant. Words that I came across included ideas, aptitude, skills, talent, power, capacity, expertise and concepts. All these things are given to you to utilise to create wealth. If you think the Lord will give you money from heaven, then that might never happen. We can't just pray and wait for someone to come and help us. The abilities are given to us for use in order to create wealth. We have to conceive the ideas, we have the aptitude, we have the power given to us, and we have the various talents endowed in us. Don't sit on your talent that God gave you utilise them.

We are cognizant of the fact that the devil was not stripped of his powers as well when he was thrown out of heaven, thus why he is capable of doing all the things that he does to this day. He also competes for souls to win over to his kingdom by offering them worldly possession. The bad part about this is that eventually you will pay back. The devil does not give for free; some sell their souls to get rich. We have heard of really dark and scary stories about celebrities who have be asked to make sacrificial killings of relatives and close friends and allies or engage in homosexual activities or join a cult in order for them to get rich and stay rich. We have also heard of victimisation that takes place if you do not agree to such term and conditions. There is always a catch when you pursue wealth using the wrong methods.

## Whose does it all belong to?
*Haggai 2 vs. 8 "The silver is mine; the gold is mine" says the LORD of host."*

But whose does it all belong to? This is a good question. We have talked about wealth and that it's not bad to be rich we also talked about the Lord giving you the strength to make wealth. We might as well consult the bible to find out who does all this gold and silver belong to. The book of Haggai says all these riches belong to the Lord God. Another bible verse also says all the things in the world are his including the beasts in the hills. Psalms 50 vs. 10-11 "For every beast of the forest are mine, and the cattle upon a thousand hills. I know all the fowls of the mountains; and the wild beasts of the field are mine" says the Lord of Host'

The context of this text highlights that God is the owner of everything. During that time there was great work of rebuilding of a temple which had been destroyed. The work required immense resources and seemed impossible. But the Lord spoke to encourage his servants to fear not and forge forward with the task. God is basically asserting his sovereignty and title as the creator and owner of the earth and all its resources. God is simply calling us to place our trust on his power and ability to supply beyond what we can imagine.

Wouldn't it be illogical if God possesses all these things but wouldn't want his children to? He can't surely be a rich father with poor kids. Parents love their children and would do anything to see their children succeed; our Father in heaven is pretty much the same, if not more. This should make us realize as his elect that nothing is beyond his reach, we need only ask and he will give us.

The decision lies with you as an individual as to what kind of life you want to live. He does not force riches on you. We choose to be rich or poor depending on the choices that we make as individuals.

## We all belong to him

***Proverbs 22 vs. 2 "The poor and the rich meet together; the Lord is the maker of them all."***

Do not be so quick to judge a book by its cover. We have established that not everyone who is wealthy is immoral. We established that one can be wealthy and still live as a straight forward and upright Christians. We also established that God also chose some rich people from the bible and worked with them, he even elevated some because of their obedience to him. It is just a matter of you choosing which side you want to belong, either the rich or the poor. Proverbs 22 vs. 2 establishes that both the rich and the poor are made by the Lord himself. Let us not despise the rich and wealthy but rather let's aspire to be as rich as they are.

When the rich and the poor meet, one group despises the other. The rich look down upon the poor and despise then for their poverty and "stupidity' while the poor despise the rich for their prosperity, "oppression of the poor" and "arrogance". But both the poor and the rich were both made by the Lord, they arrive in the world naked and leave the world without anything. The point of separation is when each group decided the path to take in terms of wealth. The objective of this proverb though is not to condemn any behaviour, but just to indicate that regardless of what one group thinks of the other, they are both made by the lord.

## He that observes the wind shall not reap

*Ecclesiastes 11.4 "He that observes the wind shall not sow and he that regards the clouds shall not reap."*

This text is as relevant in this present day and age as it was back then. One can easily get reluctant and distracted by meaningless events that happen all around us in our lives. The biblical text used an example which seemed relevant and applicable for those times since there was not as much distraction like we do in the present day.

The poor would sit and get carried away and simple stare at the clouds whilst others were busy preparing their fields and sowing. Come harvest time they did not have anything to harvest and could not put food on their tables.

The same applies to us today. We have a whole lot of things that can easily grab your attention and occupy you. Sleeping, social media and watching television are some of them. Having engaged in them for some time, take stock of what you have accomplished or if there is anything productive that you have done. More often than not it's a given that there is nothing meaning and tangible. The sad part about it is that the cycle repeats itself day in and day out. All these things are sheer wasters of productive time.

The most important aspect this verse points out is that of *the power of focus*. The thoughts and ideas that capture your attention will direct your thinking and ultimately determine your outcome. A person gravitates towards what they spend their time, energy and thoughts on. If you focus on making yourself richer rather than spending time on social media, then your will gravitate towards making it in your life. A man's harvest will depend on that which he has sown in the first place, unless you are a thief, no one reaps where they did not sow.

Some look upon the government and hope that it will address their issues. The sad truth is that governments will never be in a position to address all of your need. One of the hopes that the poor have id that the government should tax rich people or take their assets and give to the poor. The ironical part and sad truth about it is that government actually wants more people like the rich elite in order to create more jobs and solve the unemployment problem they have. In some cases governments incentivise the rich by giving them lower tax rates than individual. Furthermore businesses are taxed last after they have already incurred their expenses.

## There is equal opportunity for all

*Ecclesiastes 9 vs.11 "The race is neither to the swift, nor the battle to the strong, neither is bread to the wise, nor riches to men of understanding, nor favour to men of skill but time and chance happens to them all."*

The world around us has told us that only those that are educated, qualified, talented or experienced will get this job, have higher salaries or will make it in life. Although these maybe true to some extent, how many times have we seen people that are not educated get rich and have those that are educated and experienced work for them. The rich dad company has a book titled why A students work for C students. It is often those that are not that well educated that are working harder and often surpassing others that are more educated and qualified than they ar. Prominent examples include Facebook founder Mark Zuckerberg, Apple founder Steve Jobs, Microsoft Founder Bill Gates, Ted Turner of Turner Broadcasting Company & CNN, Larry Ellison of Oracle, Russell Simmons of Def Jam Records, Michael Dell of Dell technologies, John D Rockefeller of Standard oil and Henry Ford of ford Motor company among many others that I have skipped.

Before these people became wealthy they were just like you and me. They had the same amount of time, the same hardships that everyone else faces. Although they did not finish school, they realised that the worldly teachings of going to school and getting a job were not the right way for them. They believed in their ideas and hard work and they saw their dreams yield fruits.

A level playing field has been laid for all who want to participate and make riches for themselves and leave an inheritance for their families. Ecclesiastes says it better, it's not those that are swift or strong or wise or skilled that will make it only. Rather time and chance have been given to all of us. This implies that there is no favouritism. We all have the same 24 hours in a day and yet some seem to make it in life. Find out what it is that they are doing and do likewise. You don't have to be the most knowledgeable, strongest, smartest or the best looking to succeed. If you only depend on God's grace and work earnestly toward being a wealthy person or jus succeeding in life, you will surely achieve it. Instead of mulling over how tough the world is or how unqualified you are, just smile and think of the examples we have laid before of people who succeeded without much. Think in your mind about how the favour of the Lord is upon you.

## Heavens will open

*Deuteronomy 28 vs. 12 "The LORD will open the heavens, the storehouse of his bounty, to send rain on your land in season and to bless all the work of your hands. You will lend to many nations but will borrow from none."*

A promise is being made in this text that the Lord will send the rains in its right time. He also promises that he will bless your hand's works to the extent where your yield is abundant, this promise further goes on to state that having work with your hands and having being blessed by the lord, you will never borrow but lend.

Consider that he says you will lend to nations, this speaks to the level of wealth generated from the works of they hands. In the present day it is not hard to understand that the Lord can bless individuals and groups to the extent. If we look and wealthy individuals who have lived and some who are still with us to this present day, they have managed to amass vast wealth that exceed the national budgets of gross domestic products of other nations. Strive Masiiwa is a Zimbabwean who is popularly known on the African continent and beyond for his telecommunications businesses among others. His country has an annual budget of around US$ 1.2 billion and his net worth is beyond that. The world's richest people like Jeff Bezoz of Amazon, Warren Buffet, Bill Gates among others have accumulated wealth that is far greater than that of entire nations. J.P. Morgan in his life time was once called upon to bail out the US government. Regardless of the faith and morality of the individuals, the point is these people are in a position to assist and lend to nations if they are willing and called upon to. This is the kind of promise being given in this verse.

It is important to note that the context of the verse is indicative of the fact that the heavens are the storehouse of blessings and earth has nothing profitable until the heavens bless it. It is our responsibility to know which direction to look for these blessings and ask for them. The indispensable condition for obtaining these blessings is obedience to the word of God.

*Joshua 1 vs. 8*

*"This book of the law shall not depart from your mouth, but you shall meditate on it day and night, so that you may be careful to do according to all that is written in it; for then you will make your way prosperous, and then you will have success.*

Success brings about influence in the society around us today. If you are not a successful person you do not have any influence in any relevant issues of the day in society. Even the bible is full of examples where some prophets were not listened to because they were not successful as individuals. Thought that might not be right, the sad truth is thus how society responds to the image that we portray and how successful we are. Success attracts success. It's important to succeed because success makes you an influential person. And an influential person is the one that makes the difference.

## The first command given to Adam

*Genesis 1 vs. 28*

### "BE FRUITFUL AND MULTIPLY"

- God told Adam and Eve to "Be Fruitful And Multiply".
- Be fruitful and multiply does not just mean population wise.
- It means with plants and crops too.
- We need to respect and make wise use of the earth's natural resources.
- We need to replenish what we consume.

*"And God blessed them, and God said unto them, <u>**be fruitful**</u>, and <u>**multiply**</u>, and <u>**replenish**</u> the earth, and <u>**subdue**</u> it: and have dominion over the fish of the sea, and over the fowl of the air, and over every living thing that moveth upon the earth."*

Whether we like it or not, the most successful businesses today have managed to implement the requirements that were commanded to Adam in the above verse. Whether it was a conscious or an unconscious decision, the bottom line is they fulfilled these conditions. Take consideration of these key words.

Be fruitful – This does not mean to have children, in fact it is broader than the most common teaching we have today. This means to be productive. If you are not productive you will have difficulties making ends meet. The first command given to Adam was be productive. God didn't give Adam any shoes or any house to dwell in. They were all hidden in nature, Adam had to work and be productive to have all the essential things he needed in live.

Multiply – This simply means reproduce what has been produced. A good idea on its own does not make you wealthy, you have to be able to multiply and reproduce that idea and sell it. Steve Jobs came up with good ideas like the pc computers. IPhones, iPads and iPod were very brilliant ideas, but the ideas had to be multiplied and reproduced over and over again in order to make money. For as long as you have a good idea in your head and you do not multiply it, you will never be rich. The same iPhone 7 produced by Apple in America is reproduced in China for sale to the rest of the world. This is the same principle that God instructed to Adam, it's a shame that corporates have grasped and managed to implement this principle better than Christians. Very successful business on earth has simply followed what God had instructed and they are doing exceedingly well.

Replenish – restock, refresh, recharge or top up. These are only possible if you are distribution your products. If you do not distribute your product and have dead inventory that will destroy your success.

Subdue - to dominate, bring under control or to overcome. This is a directive from God to Adam as well, in the same verse above. It is your duty to dominate a specific area in your life as instructed above. You can choose to dominate a market and provide a product or service in that specific area and you will succeed. If you are in business and you have no intention of dominate the market, then you are probably not doing enough. Bill gates dominates computer operating software market and hence is rich

That gift that you have can be used to make you wealthy. Ask yourself what are doing with your gifts and talents? Only after doing these four requirements can we dominate the world. *Genesis 1 vs. 26*

"………*and let them have dominion over the fish of the sea, and over the fowl of the air….*" Hence dominion (verse 26) is a result realised after completing verse 28 requirements.

## Without vision people perish

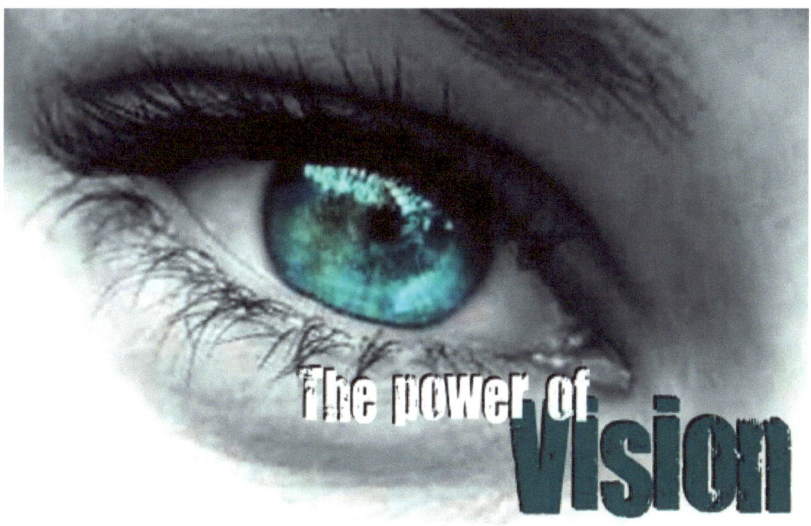

*Proverbs 29 vs. 18*

*"Where there is no vision, the people perish…."*

The most important thing we can't ever really live without in this world is a vision. The dictionary definition of vision is the ability to think about or plan the future with imagination or wisdom. It can also be phrased as a state of being able to see that which does not exist. It is seeing not what is but what can be or what should be. It may be difficult to accept this, but the truth is that what we have in our lives is largely a part of what we were able to conceive in our minds before it came to being. It does not concern itself with the past but with the future. You have got to have a vision for your relationships, your health and of course a vision for your finances.

The greatest thing about a vision is that your past mistakes do not matter. Better is the end of a thing than the beginning of it. The amount of wealth you will get in your life will be determined to a greater extent with the vision you managed to conceive in your life. Donald trump has managed to become a big real estate mogul because of his think big mantra. He has always told himself and others around him that if you are going to dream, you might as well make your dreams big. Besides being the US president he has managed to become a billionaire with real estate. He has built some very beautiful buildings because he was able to see those buildings before they existed. Steve Jobs of Apple was another example of an individual who had a vision that everyone can own a mini computer. He also envisioned beautiful products before they were even made, and he worked on making those visions a reality. The end result was people became so emotionally attached to apple products and they eagerly awaited every product launching event. They loved his ability to envision, be creative and to give them the best products in the world.

These examples of great visionaries are all around us. If you need to do further research in this area you can take a look at other people like Elon Mask who has made electric cars and space travel a practicality. Thomas Edison and his light bulb among other inventions. Henry ford of the Ford motor company. Mark Zuckerberg of Facebook. Larry Page and Sergey Brin of google. And Warren Buffet, one of the greatest investors. The list is endless. All these great people might not have known this but their ability to envision is revealed in the bible as a key to success.

God himself had a vision of what he wanted in his creation and he created it. The bible tells us in *Hebrews 11 vs 3* that ""*By faith we understand that the universe was formed at God's command, so that what is seen was not made out of what was visible.*" If God had a vision of what he wanted, we as his creations should also have a vision of what we want in all areas of our lives. It is your ability to envision that will take you far in live.

## Heaven is rich

*2 Corinthians 8 vs. 9*

*For you know the grace of our Lord Jesus Christ, that though he was rich, yet for your sake he became poor, so that you through his poverty might become rich.*

Jesus came from heaven to this earth for our redemption. More interestingly this verse is confessing that Jesus left the riches of the heavens and came to this impoverished earth so that he lift us up and become rich. These are not my words, the bible itself is saying this. As rich as he was, he chose to leave his cosy home in the heavens. His riches and wealth are as a result of the works of his hands, which reach to everything that is made, the heavens, the earth, the sea, and all that in them are, things visible and invisible; in his universal empire and dominion over all creature; and in those large revenues of glory, which are due to him from them all. Remember in the earlier sections of this book where we distinguished between riches and wealth. We concluded that these words will be used interchangeably however the reality here is God created the environment he wanted himself, thus a sign of wealth. So anything that you can think of is as a result of the works of his hands.

This testifies to the level of care the Lord has for his creation. The verse expresses that the intention, beside that of redemption is to make us rich. In other words he took our place of poverty so that we could take his place and be rich. There are many ways this verse could be interpreted but the main focus of our book is answering the question, Does God want you to be rich? So we will purposefully choose to ignore other meanings and interpretations and focus on our objective.

## God shall supply your every need
*Phil 4 Vs. 19*

*"And my God shall supply all your need according to His riches in glory by Christ Jesus."*

A promise is being made to us that we will would partake of both the spiritual and the material blessings, according to his abundant riches. All those needs be it your own or your family's need will be taken care. The problem is we might limit ourselves in our minds and set limits on what we think God can provide. The key word is ALL, not some, not a few.

## Parable of the Talents (Matthew 25 Vs 14 – 30)

The Parable of the Talents tells of a master who was leaving his house to travel, and, before leaving, entrusted his property to his servants. According to the abilities of each man, one servant received five talents, the second servant received two talents, and the third servant received one talent. The property entrusted to the three servants was worth 8 talents, where a talent was a significant amount of money.

Upon returning home, after a long absence, the master asks his three servants for an account of the talents he entrusted to them. The first and the second servants explain that they each put their talents to work. They traded and engaged in commerce in order to make a return on the talents they had been given for keep. Their investments yielded a return and they doubled the value of the property with which they were entrusted; each servant was rewarded. His master answered, 'Well done, good and faithful servants! You have been faithful with a few things. I will put you in charge of many things. Enter into the joy of your master." The third servant, however, had merely hidden his talent, had buried it in the ground, and was punished by his master for not doing anything productive with it. The third servant in Matthew's version was condemned as "wicked and lazy", for he should have deposited the talent he received with the bankers, it probably could have earned a little interest.

This is a parable as told by Jesus himself. Some of his teachings were in parables. Notice how he likens the kingdom of heaven to this parable. The interesting thing is that the only one talent which had been entrusted to him was taken away from him and given to the one who had more. Likewise God requires us to use the talents that we have got and make more from them rather than to just sit and do nothing. He is going to reward the one who makes the most from the talent entrusted to him just like in the parable. You might be disappointed if you sit doing nothing and feel sorry for yourself with the little talent you have. What you do not use you lose. That money and those resources that you have been entrusted with are to be invested, traded in order to earn a yield. It might sound like it is little to engage in trade with, that is probably the quantity deemed fit for you to start with, according to your abilities, just like in the parable. Put that money to use and see what return you will get. If he sees the good work that you have done with the little you had he will surely bless you and put you in charge of more.

## Conclusion

Having gone through his book we have gone through a number of issues that are really thought provoking. We made references to the bible as well as looked at real world examples. After doing all these what then is our conclusion therefore to this matter. Does God want you to be rich? Are rich people sinners? Should we live poor on earth so that we make it to haven? Should we only resort to prayer for our problems to be solved? Is money a sin? Hear Ye the conclusion of the matter!

We managed to establish that not all rich people are sinful people. We managed to trace bible examples for people who were rich and still found favour with God. These people include Abraham, Jacob, Isaac, Job, Solomon and Joseph among others. We too can be rich and still be obedient to God. God expects us to serve and work in his vineyard and serve others; it becomes more bearable if we have the wealth resources to expend in his work. Many wealthy people will make it to heaven if they follow what is required of them by God. Not all rich people are evil in the same way as not all poor people are righteous. Poverty is not a guarantee of virtue, and in the same manner wealth is not a guarantee of vice or moral weakness.

Money is a medium of exchange. It is used as legal tender that facilitates trade. People tend to misquote the bible and say "money is the root of all evil' this is not what the bible says. If it was so evil, then Christians should not even touch it or even get close to it if they intend to make it to heaven. So in of itself, money is not evil, but the love of love is. The only bad aspect is when you make it the master in your life and you crave for it and worship it. The bible state that when you start craving for money that is an indication of the root of evil. Money will not make you a good or bad person; rather it magnifies more of what you already are. When an unhealthy craving for money becomes the core desire, then money becomes an idol or a mini god whom all attention and 'worship' is given. Hence it can be concluded that money is an obedient servant and a bad master.

Solomon gives us an insight of how debt enslaves the borrower. Debt in the form of home equity loans, credit cards, car loans, student loans and any other borrowing for extravagant lifestyles are among the most unbearable debts that are enslaving people in the modern day society. We however established that there is good debt and bad debt, in which case good debt ids that that is used to make more money and earns a return whilst bad debt has no return but simply accumulate interest. It is not a sin but rather biblically unwise to be in debt.

A good man leaves an inheritance to his children's children. Parents are always trying to improve the lives of their children and do not want them to go through the same hardships that they grew up under. It is only honourable for good parents to want to leave something behind for their children to inherit should they pass on. Only the rich and wealthy write a will to distribute their possessions after death, poor people leave behind debts that will haunt their offspring for a long time after they are gone. If you really love your children, get a business, not a job, because when you die your children cannot inherit your job but they can definitely inherit your business.

The bible makes it clear that the Lord God himself is the one that gives the power to make wealth. It is your obligation to always remind yourself that you on your own do not have the capability to get wealth. The abilities are given to us for use in order to create wealth. We have to conceive the ideas, we have the aptitude, we have the power given to us, and we have the various talents endowed in us.

God is the creator and owner of the earth and all its resources. God is simply calling us to place our trust on his power and ability to supply beyond what we can imagine. It is illogical for God to possess all these things but wouldn't want his children to live in abundance. He can't surely be a rich father with poor kids.

But both the poor and the rich were both made by the Lord, they arrive in the world naked and leave the world without anything. The point of separation is when each group decided the path to take in terms of wealth.

The poor sit, get carried away and simple stare at the clouds whilst others were busy preparing their fields and sowing. Upon harvest they do not have anything to harvest and cannot put food on their tables. We have a whole lot of things that can easily grab your attention and occupy you. Sleeping, social media and watching television are some of them. Unless you are a thief, no one reaps where they did not sow.

A level playing field has been laid for all who want to participate and make riches for themselves and leave an inheritance for their families. It's not those that are swift or strong or wise or skilled that will make it only. Rather time and chance have been given to all of us. This implies that there is no favouritism. We all have the same 24 hours in a day and yet some seem to make it in life whilst others don't.

The first command given to Adam and Eve was <u>be fruitful</u>, and <u>multiply</u>, and <u>replenish</u> the earth, and <u>subdue</u> it: and have dominion. Being fruitful implies being productive. To multiply relates to reproduce what has been produced. Replenish is to refresh or restock after pushing volumes. Subdue means to overcome or take control over. All successful businesses have knowingly or unknowingly implemented these four principles and became rich.

The most important thing we can't ever really live without in this world is a vision. It is seeing not what is but what can be or what should be. What we have in our lives is largely a part of what we were able to conceive in our minds before it came to being. God himself had a vision of what he wanted in his creation and he created it. We too need to have a vison of the level of wealth we truly want and go achieve it. If we can't see it with our mind we can't achieve it.

God requires us to use the talents that we have got and make more from them rather than to just sit and do nothing. He is going to reward the one who makes the most from the talent entrusted to him just like in the parable. That money and those resources that you have been entrusted with are to be invested, traded in order to earn a yield. If you do not utilise them they will be taken away and given to those who know how to use them.

# The End